MW01130716

Planets in Our Solar System

URANUS

by Steve Foxe

PEBBLE
a capstone imprint

Pebble Explore is published by Pebble, an imprint of Capstone.
1710 Roe Crest Drive, North Mankato, Minnesota 56003
www.capstonepub.com

Copyright © 2021 by Capstone. All rights reserved. No part of this
publication may be reproduced in whole or in part, or stored in a retrieval
system, or transmitted in any form or by any means, electronic, mechanical,
photocopying, recording, or otherwise, without written permission of the
publisher.

**Library of Congress Cataloging-in-Publication Data is available on the
Library of Congress website.**
ISBN 978-1-9771-2397-8 (hardcover)
ISBN 978-1-9771-2697-9 (paperback)
ISBN 978-1-9771-2434-0 (eBook PDF)

Summary: Uranus is the seventh planet from the sun and has a special
feature—it tilts! Discover the mysteries of this ice giant that sits half in
darkness for more than 40 years at a time!

Image Credits
Getty Images: QAI Publishing, 23; iStockphoto: Andrew_Howe, 17; NASA:
JPL, 24, 26, 27, JPL/USGS, 22; Science Source: Julian Baum, 25, MARK
GARLICK, 5, Roger Harris, 14, TIM BROWN, 10; Shutterstock: Dotted Yeti,
Cover Left, Georgios Kollidas, 16, MattLphotography, 6–7, Mopic, 11, NASA
images, Cover, Back Cover, 1, Natalia Kirsanova, 28, Natee Jitthammachai,
9, Siberian Art, 21, Vadim Sadovski, 13, 15, 18, 19

Design Elements
Shutterstock: Arcady, BLACKDAY, ebes, LynxVector, phipatbig, Stefan
Holm, Vadim Sadovski, veronchick_84

Editorial Credits
Designer: Jennifer Bergstrom; Media Researcher: Tracy Cummins;
Production Specialist: Tori Abraham

All internet sites appearing in back matter were available and accurate
when this book was sent to press.

Printed in the United States of America.
PA117

Table of Contents

Words in **bold** are in the glossary.

Another Blue Planet

Earth has many oceans. That is why it is called the blue **planet**. Uranus is blue for a different reason. It is covered with **gases**. One gas scatters blue light.

There are eight planets in our **solar system**. Uranus is the third biggest. Only Saturn and Jupiter are larger. About 63 Earths could fit inside Uranus!

Uranus

Earth

Venus

Mars

Mercury

Earth

Jupiter

Planets in order from the sun

Uranus is very far away from the sun. It is the seventh planet from the sun. Earth is the third planet.

Sunlight takes 2 hours and 40 minutes to reach Uranus. Only Neptune is farther away.

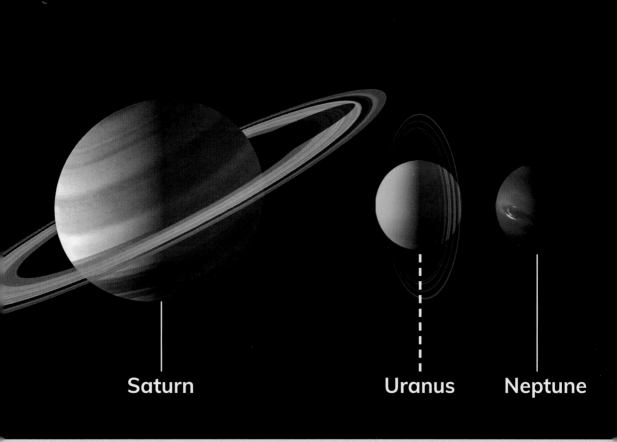

Saturn Uranus Neptune

Uranus is cold and windy.
Clouds and storms sometimes
cover the planet. The clouds have
a gas that makes them smell like
rotten eggs!

Odd Orbit, Odd Spin

Each planet moves in a circle around the sun. A planet's path is called an **orbit**. Uranus and Venus travel **clockwise** around the sun. The rest of the planets move the other way.

Earth circles the sun once a year. It takes Uranus 84 Earth years to circle the sun. That's about as long as a person's life!

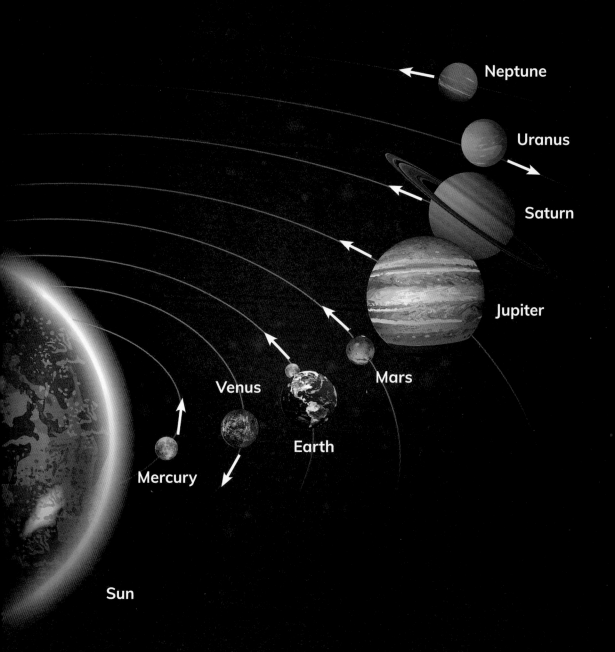

Neptune

Uranus

Saturn

Jupiter

Mars

Venus

Earth

Mercury

Sun

Arrows show direction of orbit around sun.

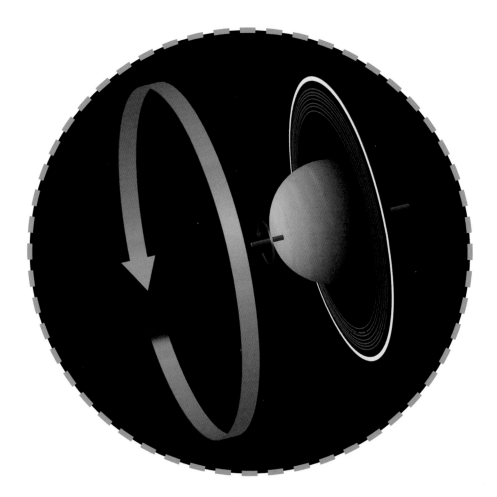

Uranus spins on its side.

Planets spin during orbit. One spin equals one day. One day on Earth is 24 hours. One day on Uranus is 17 hours and 14 minutes.

Earth spins toward the east. Uranus spins the opposite way. Uranus is the only planet that spins on its side. It does not spin like a top. It rolls like a ball. Scientists think this is because something very large hit it long ago. The crash made the planet tilt.

An object may have hit Uranus.

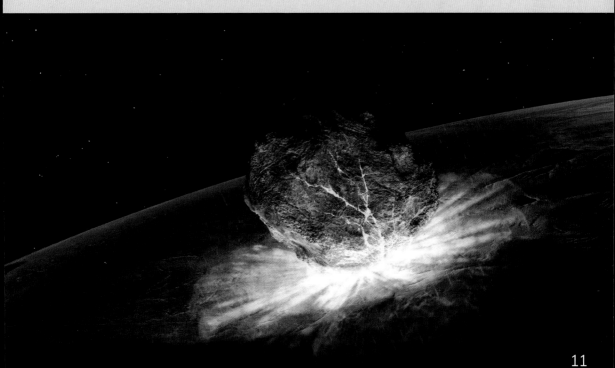

The Frosty Ice Giant

Uranus is called an **ice giant**. The ice on Uranus is not like ice on Earth. It is frozen gas. Uranus has no ground to stand on.

Planets let off heat. But Uranus does not let off much heat. The crash that made Uranus tilt may have made other changes. The planet may have lost a lot of heat then.

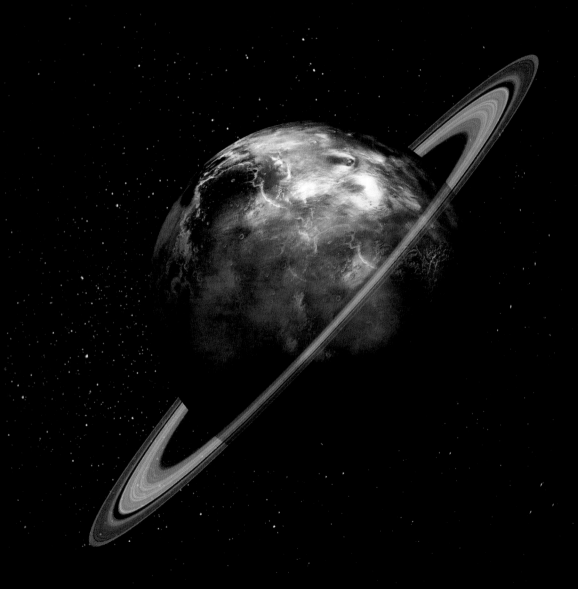

Half of Uranus stays dark a long time.

Uranus is the coldest planet. It
gets very little warmth from the sun.
Uranus can be almost three times
colder than Earth's coldest places!

Uranus also has strange seasons. Each side of the planet faces the sun for 42 Earth years at a time. Uranus has 21 years of light in summer. It has 21 years of darkness in winter! This is because of the planet's odd tilt.

Moons circling the tilted planet

Discovering a Planet

Uranus is very hard to see with the human eye. Long ago, people thought Uranus was a star. It was found using a telescope. William Herschel first saw Uranus in 1781.

William Herschel

Scientists could not agree on a name for the planet. Herschel wanted to name it after a king. A scientist named Johann Bode liked the name Uranus. In old Greek stories, Uranus is the god of the sky.

A drawing of Herschel's telescope

Some planets have rings. The planet Saturn has very large rings. Uranus also has rings. But its rings are smaller and thinner. They are difficult to see.

Saturn's rings

Rings around Uranus

Uranus has 13 rings. The rings are made of big rocks, small rocks, and dust. Some of the rings are gray in color. Others are red or blue.

Cold, Dark Moons

Uranus has 27 moons. Five of the moons are very large. They are as large as **dwarf planets**. But a moon is not a dwarf planet. A moon circles a planet. A dwarf planet circles the sun.

Herschel found the two biggest moons in 1787. Titania is the largest moon. Oberon is the next biggest. These two moons may have oceans below ice and rock.

Titania Oberon

Uranus

Uranus and its two biggest moons

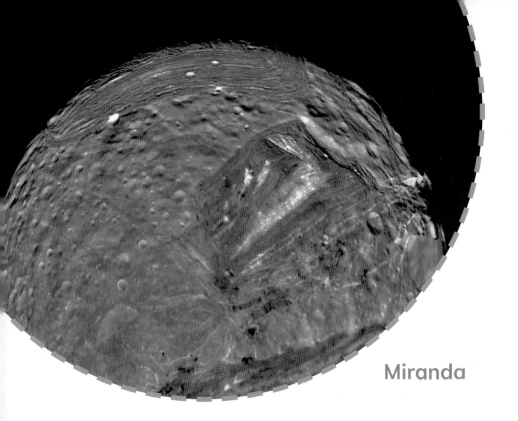

Miranda

Uranus has three other large moons. One of the moons is very dark. Another moon is very bright.

The moon named Miranda is made mostly of ice. It has many deep valleys. It also has large holes called **craters**. The tallest cliff in the solar system is on this moon.

Uranus has many smaller moons.
Most of these moons are cold and
dark. They are made of ice and rock.

Uranus and its five biggest moons

Voyager 2

Scientists send **probes** into space. These spacecraft gather information about planets and moons. A probe cannot get too close to Uranus. The swirling gases would crush it.

Voyager 2 taking off

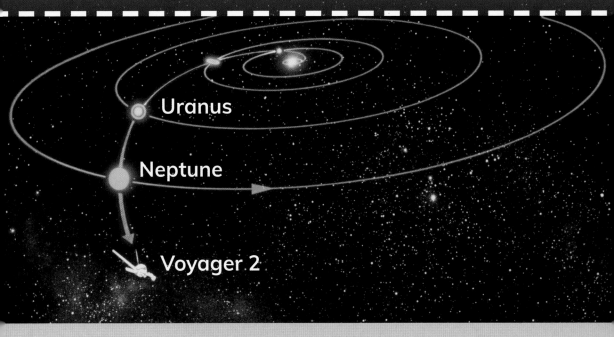

Uranus

Neptune

Voyager 2

The red line is the path of Voyager 2 as it flew past planets.

One probe has flown by Uranus. **NASA** launched Voyager 2 in 1977. It flew by Jupiter and Saturn. Then it went to Uranus and Neptune. The probe came closest to Uranus in 1986.

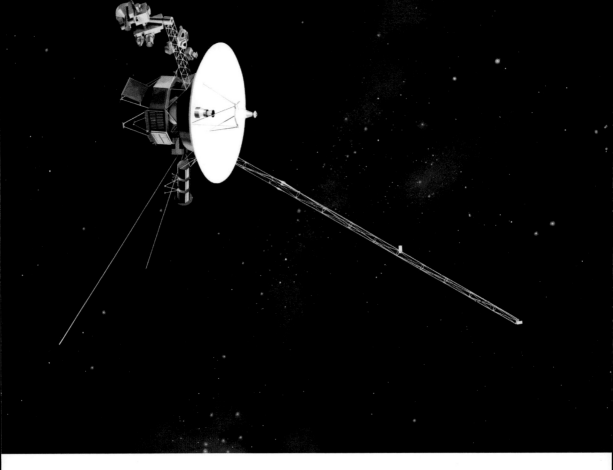

Voyager probe in space

The probe found 11 new moons of Uranus. It also sent us information about the planet's five largest moons.

The probe studied the gases that surround Uranus. It sent facts about the planet's rings to Earth. It found two new rings! It also studied the planet's sideways spin.

There are no plans to send a new probe to Uranus. But if we did, it would take about 12 years to reach the planet.

A Voyager photo of Uranus

We learned a lot about Uranus from the probe. But it only flew past Uranus. It did not circle the cold, blue planet. Maybe someday you will help us learn more about faraway Uranus!

Fast Facts

Name:
Uranus

Location:
7th from the sun

Planet Type:
ice giant

Discovered:
Astronomer William Herschel saw it with his telescope in 1781.

Moons:
27

Glossary

clockwise (KLOK-wize)—moving in the direction that the hands of a clock move

crater (KRAY-tur)—a large hole in the ground caused by crashing rocks

dwarf planet (DWORF PLA-nuht)—a large object in space that orbits the sun but is not large enough to be a planet

gas (GASS)—something that is not solid or liquid and does not have a definite shape

ice giant (ICE JIE-uhnt)—a planet made up mostly of ice

NASA (NA-suh)—National Aeronautics and Space Administration, which runs the U.S. space program

orbit (OR-bit)—the path an object follows while circling an object in space

planet (PLAN-it)—a large object that moves around a star

probe (PROHB)—a small vehicle used to explore objects in outer space

solar system (SOH-lur SISS-tum)—the sun and the objects that move around it

telescope (TEL-uh-skohp)—a tool people use to look at objects in space

Read More

Adamson, Thomas K. *The Secrets of Uranus.* North Mankato, MN: Capstone Press, 2016.

Baines, Becky. *Planets.* Washington, D.C.: National Geographic Kids, 2016.

Sommer, Nathan. *Uranus.* Minneapolis: Bellwether Media, 2019.

Internet Sites

NASA Science Solar System Exploration
https://solarsystem.nasa.gov/planets/uranus/overview/

Planets for Kids
https://www.planetsforkids.org/planet-uranus.html

European Space Agency
https://www.esa.int/kids/en/learn/Our_Universe/Planets_and_moons/Uranus

Index